JUST IN TIME ESTHER

The Book of Esther for children

Written by Carol Wedeven
Illustrated by Unada Gliewe

Arch® Books
Copyright © 1999 Concordia Publishing House
3558 S. Jefferson Avenue, St. Louis, MO 63118-3968
Manufactured in the United States of America

Xerxes called the leaders
Ruling his humongous kingdom.
Princes, lords, and generals
Paraded close behind him.

Into Xerxes' purple tent
Came thousands glad to be there.
Palace servants brought them cups
And served them all with great care.

Jews in Xerxes' Persia prayed
Their prayers to the true God.
Xerxes smiled, but Persians thought
The Jewish laws were odd.

One day Xerxes told his servants,
"I need a new wife.
Find the maiden in my land
Who fits a queenly life."

Xerxes chose dear Esther
For her beauty and sweet spirit,
Crowned her queen, gave her his heart,
And said, "Let's have a banquet!"

Esther's cousin Mordecai said,
"I bless you. Now *you* bless.
Sh-h-h-h. Take care. Don't tell them that
You really are a Jewess."

Haman was a favorite.
All bowed to Haman gladly.
But Haman was a prince with power
Who treated people badly.

Mordecai refused to bow
To Xerxes' number-two-man.
Big shot Haman raged and schemed,
Then wrote a kill-the-Jews plan:

"Kill them all and steal their things.
These hated Jews must perish."
Jews were shocked. They sat and cried
"We'll lose the lives we cherish!"

Mordecai wailed loudly,
"Save our people, queenly cousin.
Go to Xerxes. Beg for mercy.
Do not let this happen."

"I'm afraid," said Esther,
"For the king could greet or kill me,
But I'll put on my royal robes,
Be brave, and see what will be."

Xerxes told Queen Esther,
"I will give you half my kingdom."
Esther said, "Please save my people.
Let them live … in freedom."

"Who," said Xerxes, "is so cruel,
Would dare to harm or kill you?"
"*That* man plans to kill the Jews.
The name is Haman—that's who."

Haman filled with terror
As the king stood up in fury.
"Hang him!" shouted Xerxes.
When they did, that stopped the worry.

Mordecai got Haman's job
And changed the nasty order.
Jews were saved in every place
Within the Persian border.

Now each year Jews celebrate
The girl who grew up braver.
She was born to do a job,
To be a people-saver.

Dear Parents:

A picture of God's grace to us is painted in this Old Testament story. Queen Esther is willing to die for her people and stands as their advocate in order to save them. God sent His Son, Jesus, to be our advocate and to die for our sins so that we might be saved eternally.

It was important that the Jewish people be saved so that the Redeemer-Messiah could be born to God's chosen people. God worked through Esther, an ordinary person, to overcome impossible obstacles so that His gracious will might be accomplished.

Esther placed her trust in God as she stood up to Haman and requested that King Xerxes save her people. There will be times when our children must place their trust in God so that they might stand up for their beliefs. Consider how you might model this type of trust for your children to see. God also works through you to accomplish His purposes.

The Editor